Life around the World

Families in Many Cultures

Revised Edition

by Heather Adamson

Consulting Editor: Gail Saunders-Smith, PhD

CAPSTONE PRESS
a capstone imprint

Pebble Plus is published by Capstone Press,
1710 Roe Crest Drive, North Mankato, Minnesota 56003.
www.mycapstone.com

Copyright © 2008, 2016 by Capstone Press, a Capstone imprint. All rights reserved.
No part of this publication may be reproduced in whole or in part, or stored in a retrieval system, or transmitted in any form or by any means, electronic, mechanical, photocopying, recording, or otherwise, without written permission of the publisher. For information regarding permission, write to Capstone Press,
1710 Roe Crest Drive, North Mankato, Minnesota 56003.

Library of Congress Cataloging-in-Publication Data is available on the Library of Congress website.
ISBN 978-1-5157-3695-0 (revised paperback)

Editorial Credits
Sarah L. Schuette, editor; Alison Thiele, set designer; Kara Birr, photo researcher

Photo Credits
Capstone Press: 4, 6, 8, 10, 12, 14, 18, 20; Getty Images: Eco Images, 15, Simon Marcus, 17; iStockphoto: Chris Johnson, Cover, Cliff Parnell, 21, monkeybusinessimages, 7, Rich Legg, 11; Shutterstock: ChameleonsEye, 9, Jason Stitt, 1, meunierd, 5, Steve Vidler, 13; Superstock: Wolfgang Kaehler, 19

Note to Parents and Teachers

The Life around the World set supports national social studies standards related to culture and geography. This book describes and illustrates families in many cultures. The images support early readers in understanding the text. The repetition of words and phrases helps early readers learn new words. This book also introduces early readers to subject-specific vocabulary words, which are defined in the Glossary section. Early readers may need assistance to read some words and to use the Table of Contents, Glossary, Read More, Internet Sites, and Index sections of the book.

Printed in the United States 5657

Table of Contents

Living Together 4
Around the House 10
Family Fun 14
Your Family 20

Glossary 22
Read More 23
Internet Sites 23
Index 24

Living Together

Families of all sizes
live around the world.
How is your family
like other families?

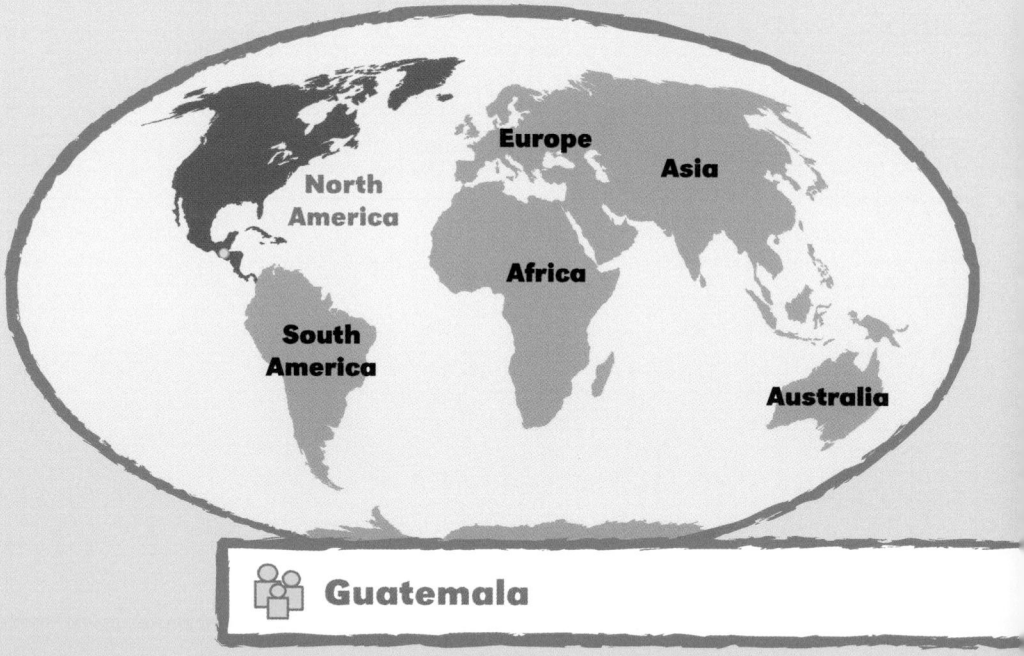

Children around the world
live with their parents.
Sometimes grandparents
live with them too.

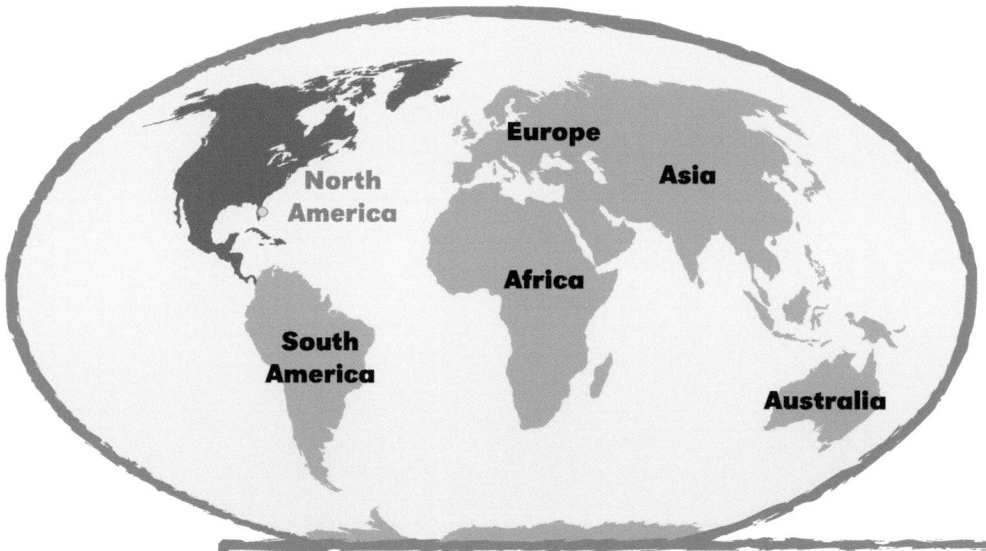

United States of America

Aunts, uncles, and cousins
are parts of families too.
They may live far away.

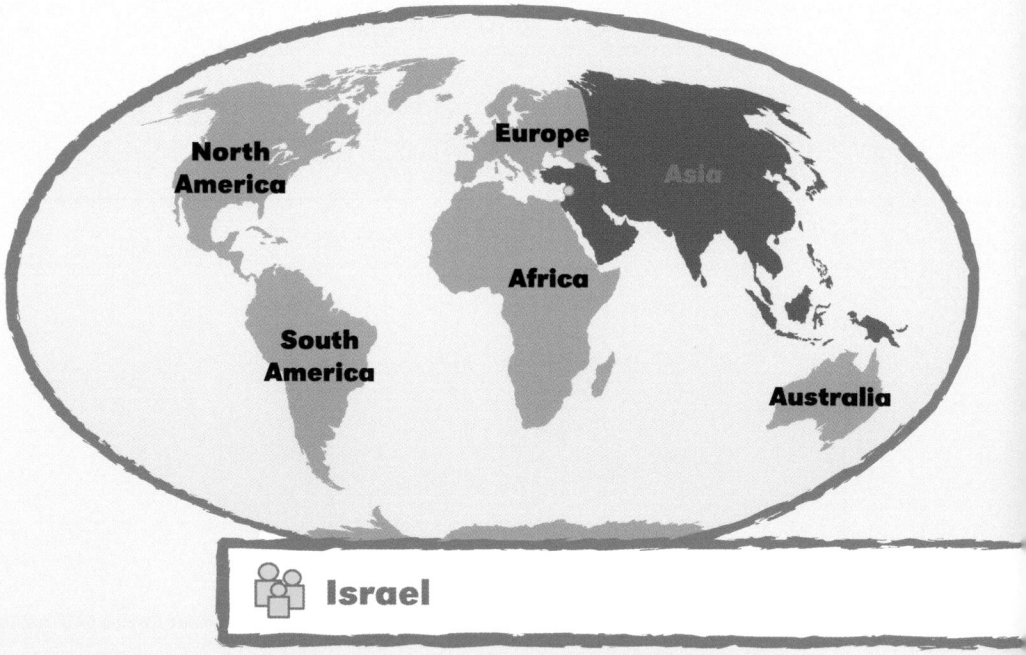

Around the House

Families help each other.
A mother in China
helps her son
with homework.

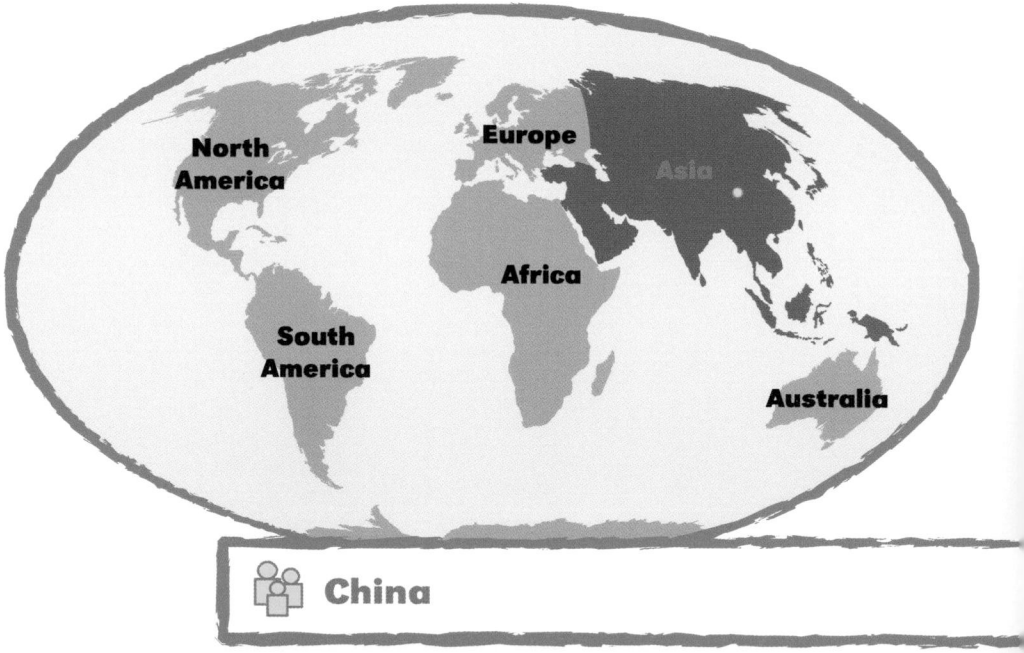

Families share meals.
A family in New Zealand
cooks and eats together.

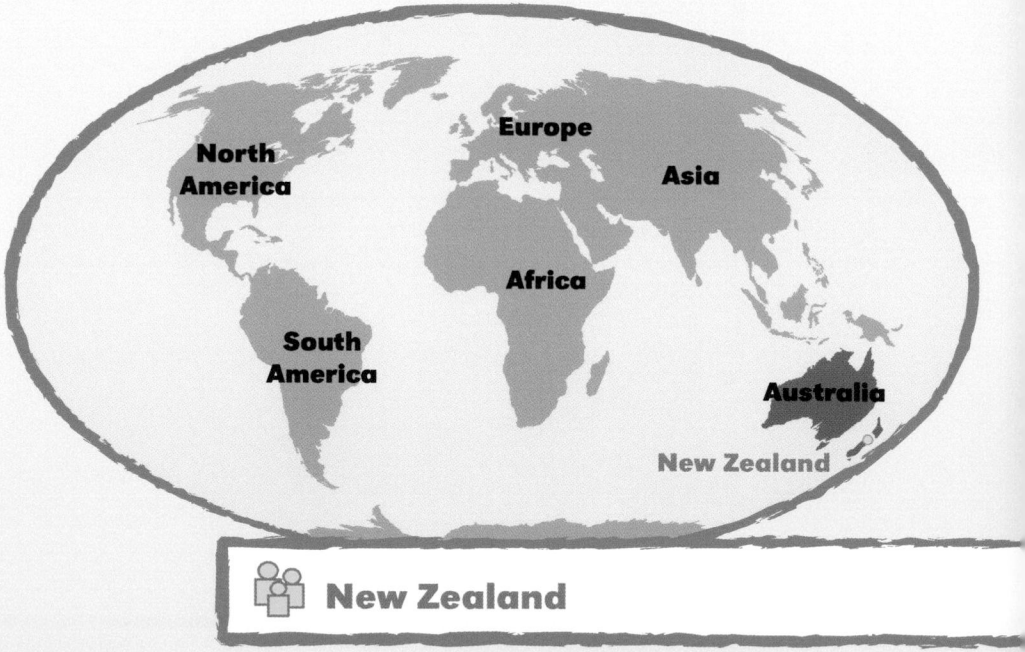

New Zealand
KIWI COOK OF THE YEAR!
ORIGINAL
OUTDOOR ADVENTURE
Cook-In

Family Fun

Families celebrate holidays.
A family in Africa dances
and visits with relatives.

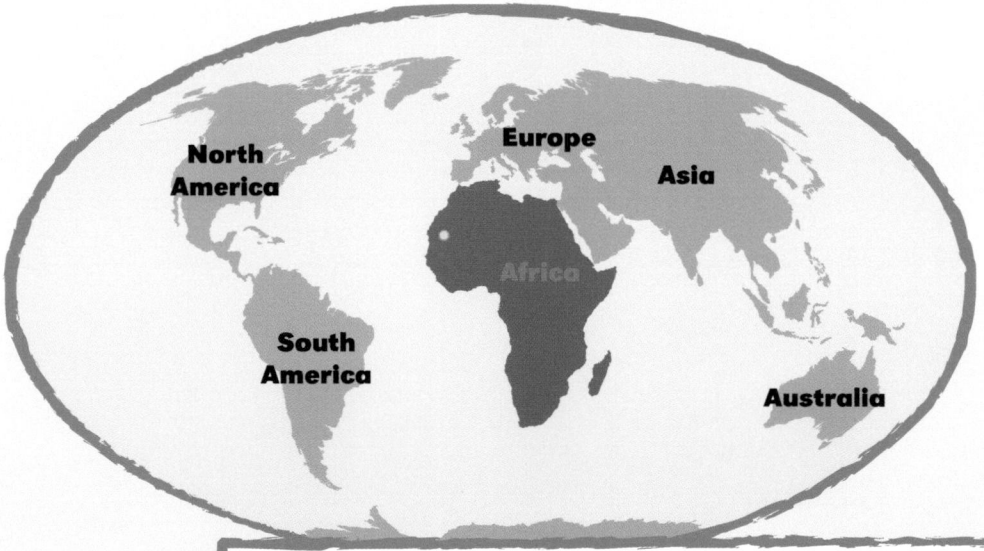

Mauritania

Families celebrate birthdays.
A father in China blows out
his birthday candles.

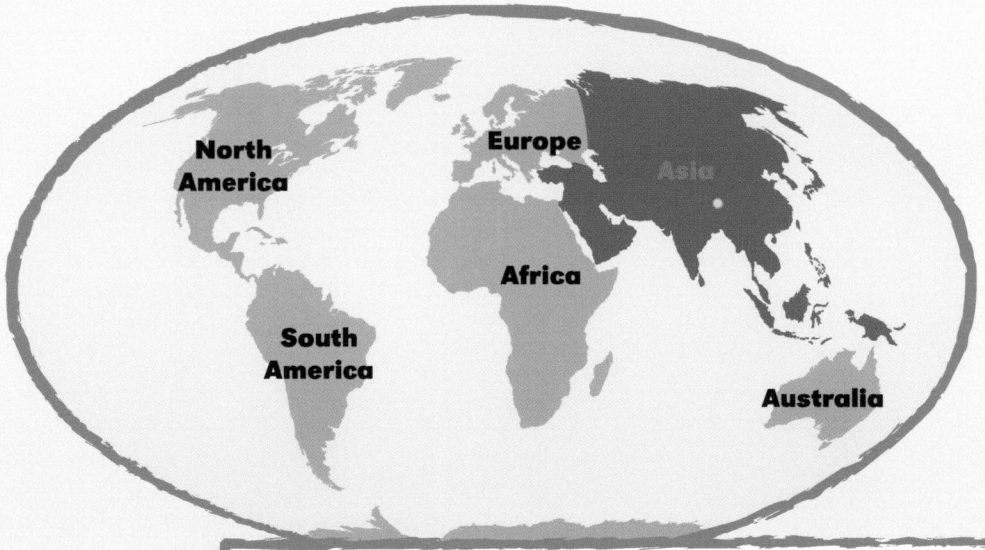

China

Families play together.
A family in Germany surfs
on their vacation.

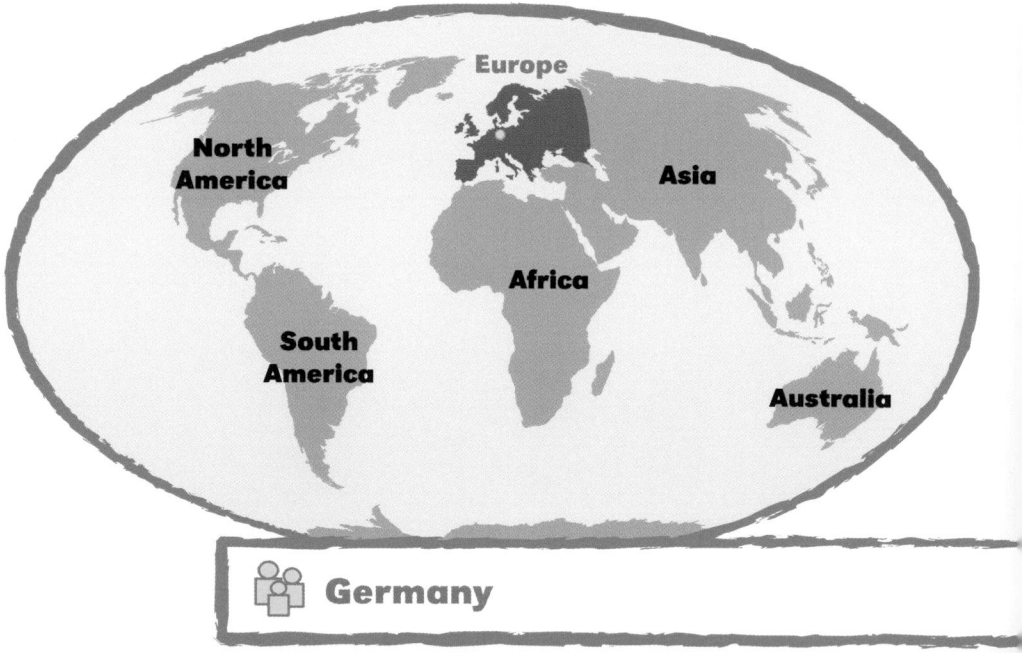

Your Family

Families hug
and laugh together.
How does your family
have fun?

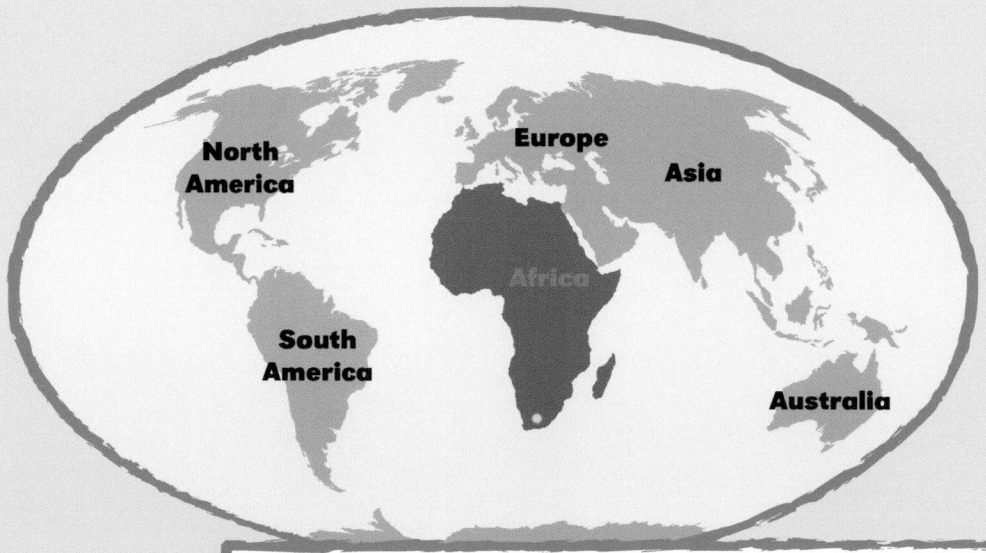

South Africa

Glossary

celebrate—to do something fun on a special occasion; families often gather together to celebrate birthdays, holidays, or other important events.

holiday—a festival, religious celebration, or day of memory

meal—the food that is served and eaten at certain times of the day such as breakfast or lunch

relative—a member of your family; your parents, grandparents, aunts, uncles, and cousins are relatives.

surf—to ride on waves using a surfboard

vacation—a time of rest from school, work, or a trip away from home

Read More

Easterling, Lisa. *Families.* Our Global Community. Chicago: Heinemann, 2007.

Kuklin, Susan. *Families.* New York: Hyperion Books, 2006.

Robertson, J. Jean. *Meet My Grandparents.* Vero Beach, Fla.: Rourke, 2007.

Internet Sites

FactHound offers a safe, fun way to find Internet sites related to this book. All of the sites on FactHound have been researched by our staff.

Here's how:

1. Visit *www.facthound.com*
2. Choose your grade level.
3. Type in this book ID **1429600195** for age-appropriate sites. You may also browse subjects by clicking on letters, or by clicking on pictures and words.
4. Click on the **Fetch It** button.

FactHound will fetch the best sites for you!

Index

aunts, 8
birthdays, 16
celebrating, 14, 16
children, 6
cooking, 12
cousins, 8
eating, 12
fathers, 16
grandparents, 6
helping each other, 10
holidays, 14
meals, 12
mothers, 10
parents, 6
parties, 16
playing, 18
relatives, 14
sons, 10
uncles, 8
vacations, 18

Word Count: 114
Grade: 1
Early-Intervention Level: 12